weblinks

You don't need a computer to use this book. But, for readers who do have access to the Internet, the book provides links to recommended websites which offer additional information and resources on the subject.

You will find weblinks boxes like this on some pages of the book.

weblinks

For more information on alternative fuels, go to www.waylinks.co.uk/series/ susworld/transport

waylinks.co.uk

To help you find the recommended websites easily and quickly, weblinks are provided on our own website, **waylinks.co.uk.** These take you straight to the relevant websites and save you typing in the Internet address yourself.

Internet safety

↗ Never give out personal details, which include: your name, address, school, telephone number, email address, password and mobile number.

↗ Do not respond to messages which make you feel uncomfortable – tell an adult.

↗ Do not arrange to meet in person someone you have met on the Internet.

↗ Never send your picture or anything else to an online friend without a parent's or teacher's permission.

↗ If you see anything that worries you, tell an adult.

A note to adults
Internet use by children should be supervised. We recommend that you install filtering software which blocks unsuitable material.

Website content

The weblinks for this book are checked and updated regularly. However, because of the nature of the Internet, the content of a website may change at any time, or a website may close down without notice. While the Publishers regret any inconvenience this may cause readers, they cannot be responsible for the content of any website other than their own.

HODDER
Wayland

SUSTAINABLE WORLD

TRANSPORT

Rob Bowden

HODDER
Wayland

An imprint of Hodder Children's Books

SUSTAINABLE WORLD

Energy • Environments • Food and Farming
Transport • Urbanization • Waste

Sustainable World: Transport

Copyright © 2003 Rob Bowden
First published in 2003 by Hodder Wayland,
an imprint of Hodder Children's Books.

Commissioning Editor: Victoria Brooker
Book Designer: Jane Hawkins
Consultant: Rodney Tolley

Book Editor: Margot Richardson
Picture Research: Shelley Noronha, Glass Onion Pictures

Series concept by: Environment and Society International –
Educational Resourcing

British Library Cataloguing in Publication Data
Bowden, Rob
  Transport. - (The sustainable world)
  1. Transportation - environmental aspects - Juvenile literature
  I. Title
  388
  ISBN 075 023 9867

Printed in Hong Kong by Wing King Tong

Hodder Children's Books
A division of Hodder Headline Limited
338 Euston Road, London NW1 3BH

Cover: A cyclist avoids the traffic by choosing an alternative transport option.
Title page: Separate traffic lanes in Amsterdam encourage the use of more sustainable forms of transport.
Contents page: Traffic in Burkina Faso, Africa.

Picture Acknowledgements
Cover: Jim Erickson/Corbis
Camera Press (Darren Jacklin) 8; James Davis Photography 37;
EASI-Images (Rob Bowden) 12, 15, 31; Ecoscene (Nick Hawkes)
19, 30, (PJ) 33, (Adrian Morgan) 34; Eye Ubiquitous (Paul Scheult) 23;
Impact (Caroline Penn) 3, (Piers Cavendish) 10, (Mark Henley) 15, (Stewart
Weir) 18, (Mark Henley) 25, (Mark Henley) 32, (Philippe Achache) 42; Mouchel
Consultants (Safer Routes to School Team) 40; Popperfoto
(Reuters/Beawiharta) 7, (Reuters/Regis Duvignau) 12, Popperfoto (Reuters)
24, (Reuters/Greg Bos) 36, (Reuters/Marcelo Del Pozo) 38, Margot Richardson
28; Still Pictures (Mark Edwards) 1, (Mark Edwards) 4, (Shehzad Nooran) 5,
(Mark Edwards) 9, (Mark Edwards) 11, (Mark Edwards) 16 (top), (Mark Edwards)
16-17 (bottom), (Mark Edwards) 17, (Mark Edwards) 20, (Jorgen Schytte) 21,
(Ron Giling) 26, (John Maier) 27, (Mark Edwards) 29, (Dylan Garcia) 35,
(Mark Edwards) 39, (Reinhard Janke) 41, (Thomas Raupach) 44, (Thomas Raupach)
45; Topham (Bob Daemmrich/The Image Works) 13, (Image Works) 22; Toyota Cars
14; Wayland (Jimmy Holmes) 6, 43.

Contents

Why sustainable transport?

WE LIVE IN A WORLD WHERE MOBILITY is an essential part of our lives. Every day we make journeys: to school or to work; to the shops; to entertainment or leisure facilities; and to visit friends and family. Some of these journeys are local, while others cover great distances. What is increasingly common to all of our journeys, however, is that we use some form of transport to make them. Our decision to use transport and our choice of transport type are of great importance to the state of our environment, and to our health and well-being.

Los Angeles' freeways are among the busiest roads in the world.

THINK FIRST

You may not think hard about your transport choices, but there are good reasons to do so. For example, transport is the fastest growing source of carbon-dioxide emissions that contribute to climate change. Congestion caused by transport causes ill health and premature death for millions of people every year. And road traffic accidents kill up to one million people a year, most of them pedestrians. Transport is also one of the fastest growing industries. The number of cars alone is expected to double between now and 2010 to over one billion! Such trends show that there are real reasons to be concerned about transport and its impact on people and the environment.

These cycle rickshaws in Bangladesh are a sustainable form of transport because they use human energy for power.

DATABANK

In 1970 there was approximately one car for every eighteen people. By 2001 this had grown to one car for every twelve people and by 2010 it could reach one for every seven people.

ALTERNATIVE CHOICES

The future of transport need not follow the trends of the last fifty years. There are alternatives. Many countries and individuals are now choosing to create more sustainable transport: that is, transport that does not cause harm to others or to the environment, both now and in the future. For example, walking is a completely sustainable method of transport because it uses only human energy and produces no pollutants. Car use by contrast, is often completely unsustainable as it uses non-renewable fossil fuels and is very polluting. The sustainability of other transport alternatives such as cycling, trams and buses lies somewhere in between the extremes of walking and car use.

Central to the success of alternatives is choice: people must choose sustainable transport for themselves. But to do this, they must understand the problems of existing transportation and their options for the future. This book introduces some of those problems and presents options that will allow you to make better transport choices for a sustainable world.

The transport problem

Vehicles in less developed countries, such as Pakistan, are often adapted to carry as much as possible because motorized transport is very scarce.

TRANSPORT IS OFTEN considered vital for the progress and development of a country or region. Getting to basic services such as schools or hospitals can be difficult in areas where transport facilities are lacking. In northern Kenya, for example, a lack of transport means people may have to walk over 50 km to reach their nearest health centre and up to 15 km per day to attend school. Where transport has been improved, local communities have often benefited: trade links and people's opportunities have been increased. For example, in Morocco, improvements to rural roads increased agricultural trade dramatically and more than doubled school and hospital attendances within just a few years.

A SECOND LOOK

Transport provision is not always positive, however. The benefits of some forms of transport are now increasingly outweighed by their costs, including pollution, congestion and accidents. For example, in Asia it is estimated that 1.56 million people die each year due to

These Indonesian children are wearing face masks to protect themselves from smog and smoke in busy traffic.

atmospheric pollution, much of which comes from motorized transport such as cars and buses. In the USA, meanwhile, up to two billion hours are wasted each year by people stuck in urban traffic jams and in the UK around 40,000 people are killed or seriously injured each year by accidents on the roads. Such costs have led many people to question the benefits of some transport systems. For them, it is time to take a second look at our transport options.

Many experts are concerned about the growing dependence on motor vehicles all over the world. Today, motor vehicles are the favoured form of transport for most people living in more developed, industrialized countries (North America, Europe, Japan, etc). In Western Europe for example, the number of passenger cars more than doubled between 1970 and 1995, whilst road freight tripled. Motor transport is also increasing rapidly in less developed regions as economies grow and incomes rise. Asia and Latin America have particularly fast growth, but in Africa car use is rising only slowly.

CAR MANIA

So why is motor transport, and particularly the car, so popular? Well, for one thing, cars have become relatively cheap over the years as improvements in technology have reduced manufacturing costs and improved vehicle efficiency. But cars have also become something of a status symbol, often seen as a sign of wealth and success. In some societies they are almost fashion accessories with people changing their model or colour as tastes change. Take the latest trend in the USA for sport utility vehicles (SUVs), for example. In 1975, SUVs accounted for 20 per cent of new car sales in the USA, but by 1999 this had risen to 46 per cent. Such

Some cars, such as this convertible in Florida, USA, are treated more as a fashion accessory than a form of transport.

trends are encouraged by advertising and the motor industry spends more than any other on advertising – nearly $US24 billion in 1998, over $US14 billion of which was in the USA alone!

People believe that owning a car brings them freedom and opportunities; that they can go anywhere at any time. Car ownership has become a rite of passage in many countries with teenagers counting down the days until they get behind the wheel and earn their freedom. This feeling is so strong that in one UK survey nearly three-quarters of young adults felt that the right to a driving licence was more important than the right to vote! This obsession with the car has led some transport experts to describe it as 'car mania'.

> ## OPINION
>
> As I sit in traffic, windows rolled up against the fumes from idling exhausts, I wonder what happened to the freedom I once enjoyed.
>
> *Jim Motavalli, Sierra Magazine 1999*

The air around Mexico City airport is thick with smog and pollution. Aircraft pollution is worse at altitude though.

SKY HIGH

Another transport problem is the growth in air travel. Since 1960, air travel around the world has increased by around 9 per cent per year. By 2010 it is estimated that one billion people (15 per cent of the world total) will be travelling by air each year. Air freight has increased even faster at around 11 per cent per year. The problem is that air travel is very polluting. A passenger flying for eight hours contributes as much to global warming as an average person in India does in a year. With air travel set to grow dramatically the environmental costs could be sky high in the future.

RAILWAYS IN DECLINE

Car and air travel have increasingly replaced rail as a form of transport and so railways have, in many countries, declined in importance. In Kenya, Mexico and South Africa, for example, rail travel declined by over 50 per cent between 1980 and 2000. In other countries, including the UK, Japan and France, the railway network has declined in size too. In the USA, the rail network shrank by nearly 40 per cent between 1980 and 2000 from 265,842 kilometres of track to 159,822 kilometres. The decline of railways is of particular concern because they are a more efficient and sustainable form of transport than air or road travel. For example, over distances of less than 500 kilometres, rail travel produces three times less carbon dioxide than air travel.

UNEQUAL ACCESS

Of course, transport problems are not limited to the type of transport chosen. On a global scale there is the problem of unequal access to transport. Whilst most people living in more developed nations are spoiled for choice, for many people in less developed countries there is little choice at all. For example, many women walk for over an hour and a half each day on essential journeys such as collecting water or fuel-wood for their families. They may carry weights of over 20 kilograms (often on their heads) and walk for several kilometres on each trip. For these women, and millions of others like them, the lack of transport is a much

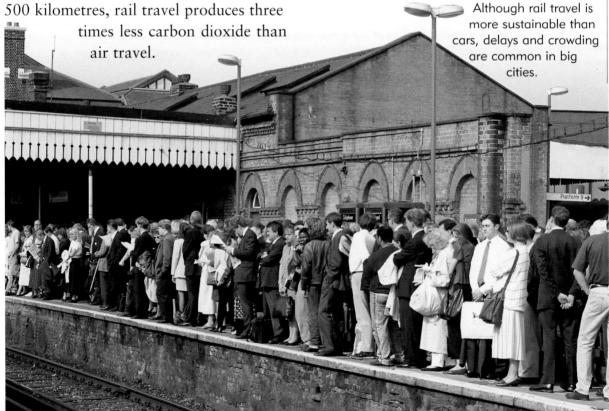

Although rail travel is more sustainable than cars, delays and crowding are common in big cities.

With limited access to affordable transport, millions of people, such as these women in Africa, have only their own power to carry heavy loads.

bigger problem than the type of transport chosen. Even where transport does exist it is not always affordable. For example, in Manila, the capital of the Philippines, the poorest residents may spend up to 14 per cent of their income just to travel to work.

THE ROAD AHEAD?

People who currently lack transport need reliable, safe and cheap forms of transport to improve their quality of life and well-being. But, as many experts now agree, the model followed by the more developed nations – roads and car-mania – is not a solution. Instead, people need to think afresh and develop innovative and sustainable transport solutions for the future. Such thinking will also have to occur in the more developed nations if the hope of a more sustainable world is to be turned into a reality.

DATABANK

Industrial nations use 59 per cent of global transportation energy, despite having just 19 per cent of the world population.

Traffic accidents kill around 885,000 people per year – equivalent to 10 jumbo jets crashing every day with no survivors!

Developing sustainable transport

ALTHOUGH THINKING ABOUT SUSTAINABLE transport may be new for many people, some of the ideas and technology involved go back many years. For example, the light railways now being introduced into many urban centres are similar to tram systems that were first introduced in 1860 in London.

Similarly, electric cars, which are now on the verge of a comeback, originated in the late 1880s and in the USA were as popular as petrol vehicles until around 1920. Bicycles have an even longer history, dating back to 1791 and are still one of the most sustainable forms of transport. Despite this long history, sustainable transport systems have yet to be fully developed and are now relatively few and far between.

EFFICIENCY GAINS

To date, most of the effort towards creating sustainable transport has been in the improvement

Top: An old trolleybus still runs in Birkenhead, UK, though it is now mainly a tourist attraction.

Left: A mechanic checks bikes in Bordeaux, France. These were loaned free of charge to the public to promote ecology-friendly transport in the city.

SELF

DATABANK

Motor vehicles in the USA produce more global-warming pollutants than all of the sources in Great Britain combined.

of existing transport options, particularly the efficiency of the motor car. This concern developed following a sudden increase in the cost of oil during the 1970s. By 1980 the price of crude oil (from which petrol and diesel are derived) was ten times higher than in 1973. Several governments introduced measures encouraging manufacturers to make more fuel-efficient vehicles as a result. For example, the USA introduced the Corporate Average Fuel Economy (CAFE) programme in 1975. The CAFE programme sets average fuel-efficiency targets for new vehicles made by motor manufacturers. If a manufacturer fails to meet these targets it is fined by the government. Partly as a result of such measures, an average US family car today uses half the fuel of one built in 1975.

The CAFE levels are currently set at 27.5 miles per US gallon (mpg) for passenger cars and 20.7 mpg for vans and light trucks (including SUVs), but some campaigners believe these are not high enough. They claim that if CAFE standards were raised to 45 mpg for cars and 34 mpg for light trucks carbon dioxide emissions would be cut by 600 million tons per year and the US would save around 3 million barrels of oil per day! The technology to meet such standards already exists, but in recent years the fuel efficiency of US manufacturers has actually been falling due to consumer preference for bigger 'gas guzzling' vehicles.

The Toyota Prius contains both an electric motor and a petrol engine. It aims to reduce emissions in urban driving and to give greater fuel efficiency.

TECHNOLOGY SOLUTIONS

Most improvements in the fuel efficiency of motor vehicles have come about through improved vehicle technology. Lightweight materials, such as aluminium and plastics, mean that vehicles are much lighter than in the past, but still as strong and safe. As weight is reduced the engine operates more efficiently. In fact, for every 10 per cent reduction in weight, fuel efficiency increases by almost 6 per cent. Other changes in car design have also improved fuel efficiency dramatically: better engines, improved tyres, modern gearboxes and better aerodynamics have all reduced the amount of fuel used. Despite this, experts suggest that the efficiency of many vehicles could be improved further by over 50 per cent.

DATABANK

Only about 15 per cent of the energy in fuel is actually used to move our vehicles. Most is lost as heat, or due to mechanical, road and wind resistance.

CLEANER FUELS

The majority of motor vehicles are fuelled by petrol or diesel derived from oil. Oil is a non-renewable resource that is fast being used up in an energy-hungry world. Oil-based fuels are also very polluting. Their waste emissions contribute to climate change, acid rain, urban smog and numerous health problems for humans.

One of the most serious health issues has been the use of lead in petrol. Lead is toxic to humans and builds up in the body

Exhaust fumes contribute to the acid rain that has eroded details from this stone plaque in Stockholm, Sweden.

causing paralysis, blindness, brain damage and even death. In more developed countries lead has been phased out of petrol since the 1970s, but in many less developed regions it is still used. In some of Africa's major cities, for example, up to 90 per cent of children suffer from lead poisoning. Another major pollutant, sulphur, has also been drastically reduced in modern fuels. Sulphur that is released into the atmosphere contributes to acid rain, but the cleaner fuels now available have reduced emissions by up to 90 per cent.

Cleaner fuels are not all good news, however. They still use oil and encourage car use. In more recent years some of the chemicals used in cleaner fuels have also become a cause for concern. In unleaded petrol, for example, an additive called MTBE (methyl tertiary butyl ether) that helps engines run smoothly and reduces air pollution is thought to have links with cancer in humans and of having a damaging effect on wildlife. In the UK, MTBE has been blamed for a reduction in the number of house sparrows, one of the UK's most common birds.

Congested roads and poor quality vehicles, as here in Calcutta, India, can lead to high levels of air pollution.

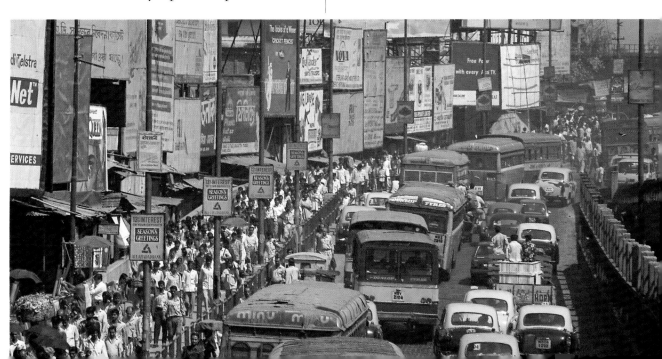

ALTERNATIVE FUELS

Concern about oil-based fuels has led to several alternatives being developed. Plant extracts have formed a particular focus of attention. In Brazil, for example, 40 per cent of motor vehicles run on pure ethanol made from sugar cane, whilst the remainder run on a blend of ethanol (22 per cent) and petrol (78 per cent). Bio-diesel is another plant-based fuel (made from vegetable oils) that is on the increase as both a pure and blended fuel. Bio-diesel is of particular interest because it can be used in existing diesel engines without them being modified. Plant-based fuels are renewable and release far fewer pollutants than oil-based fuels. However, they still release carbon dioxide – one of the most serious pollutants.

One alternative fuel now under development that releases no pollutants whatsoever is hydrogen fuel. By combining hydrogen with oxygen in a

Sugar cane is one crop used to make a less polluting and sustainable form of vehicle fuel.

special fuel cell it is possible to generate electricity for powering a vehicle and the only waste is clean, drinkable water. The problem is how to make the hydrogen. At the moment it is mainly produced from conventional fossil fuels and is therefore still polluting. It is possible to produce hydrogen from water, though, with oxygen as the only waste product. If the energy for hydrogen production came from renewable sources such as the wind or the sun then it would be possible to have near pollution-free motoring.

— **weblinks** —

For more information on alternative fuels, go to:
www.waylinks.co.uk/series/susworld/transport

Trams, cyclists and pedestrians in Amsterdam, the Netherlands, show that transport need not depend on the car.

BEYOND THE CAR

Improved vehicle efficiency and new fuels are undoubtedly making transport more sustainable, but they are still focused on individual motor vehicles. The more sustainable projects are those that try to move beyond our reliance on the car. Light rail systems, for example, now provide a clean and efficient transport option in an increasing number of cities. The most modern light rail systems can carry up to 20,000 people per hour. To carry the same number of people by road would need a 15-lane highway! Cycle lanes have also been given greater priority in recent years. In Copenhagen, Denmark a quarter of all city journeys are made by bicycle.

DATABANK

Six bicycles typically fit into the road space used by one car. For parking, 20 bicycles occupy the space required for a single car.

A motorist in Brazil fills his car with 'alcool', a fuel based on ethanol that is extracted from sugar cane.

Park and Ride schemes provide out-of-town car parks. Drivers then travel into urban centres on public transport, reducing congestion and pollution.

DESIGNED FOR LIFE

In European towns and cities up to a quarter of urban space is taken up by traffic. In Los Angeles, USA – the car capital of the world – an incredible two-thirds of land is used for roads and car parks. Such shocking figures have led many to call for a return to cities that are designed for life, not traffic! Throughout the world, town centres are being closed to traffic and returned to people. The impact this has on sustainable transport is significant. In Strasbourg, France, for example, the banning of cars from the city centre has led to bicycle use five times higher than in French cities where cars still have access. In Oxford, in the UK, daytime traffic went down by 63 per cent following restrictions to limit all but essential traffic from entering the city centre. At the same time, improved buses and Park and Ride schemes still allow people to reach the city for business or shopping. Such schemes are likely to become more commonplace in the future.

PREPARED TO PAY

One approach to sustainable transport has been to charge higher prices for those forms that are less sustainable. In Singapore, for example, an electronic road-pricing system automatically charges motorists using busy or congested roads. This encourages them to use public transport instead and so reduces congestion and saves the driver money. As a result of this and other transport policies, 63 per cent of all motorized journeys in Singapore are made by public transport. Road pricing is also common in France on some of its main roads and in the UK, motorists have had to pay to drive into central London since the introduction of congestion charges in February 2003.

ROLE MODELS

Central to the development of sustainable transport is the need for people to see how such a future might look and work. Without successful examples people may be reluctant to give up their current transport choice. Two good role models are the cities of Freiburg in Germany and Curitiba in Brazil. Since the early 1970s both cities have developed transport policies that are widely recognized as some of the most sustainable in the world. We'll consider these and other successful examples of sustainable transport in the next chapter.

Road tolls, such as these on France's autoroutes, can help reduce traffic levels if they are correctly priced to discourage car use.

Sustainable transport in practice

THE INTEREST IN NEW FUELS and efficient technology is seen by many environmentalists as something of a false hope for sustainable transport. They do not question that the doubling of fuel efficiency is of great benefit and that cleaner fuels are helping to clean our air. But what, they question, is the benefit of such measures if there are simply more and more motorized vehicles being used and more and more miles being travelled in them? The real future of sustainable transport, so say most environmentalists, will depend on greater use of public transport and zero-emission options such as bicycles and walking.

These separate traffic lanes in Amsterdam, the Netherlands, help to encourage more sustainable forms of transport.

Privately owned *matatus* (mini buses) wait to fill up before going to various city centre destinations in Kampala, Uganda.

GOING PUBLIC?

Public transport plays an important role in most countries, though this varies dramatically across the world. For example, in Japan around 46 per cent of motorized journeys are currently made by some form of public transport, whereas in the USA it is just 2 per cent! In less developed countries where incomes are generally much lower, public transport is often the main or only form of motorized transport available to people. In East Africa, for example, local minibuses or pick-up trucks, known as *matatus*, are the main form of motorized transport with bigger buses operating only on intercity routes.

Throughout the world, however, there has been a trend towards less use of public transport. This is because incomes have risen and personal car use has grown. In South Korea, for example, a tripling of incomes between 1980 and 1995 saw the number of privately owned motor vehicles increase by an amazing 2,216 per cent. As fewer people use public transport, routes and frequency are reduced and vehicles fall into disrepair. This in turn makes public transport less attractive and may persuade those using it to use their own vehicles instead. In rural areas of the UK and on the outskirts of many towns such trends led to a virtual collapse of bus services that until the mid-1950s were the main form of passenger transport. (Today, buses account for just 6 per cent of UK passenger journeys.) In recent years, however, congestion and concern about the environment have been slowly changing attitudes towards public transport.

DATABANK

There were 532 million cars in use globally in 2000. This is twice as many as in 1975 and ten times the number in 1950.

A previously abolished train service returns to New York state, USA.

GROWING DEMAND

Many countries are currently experiencing a growth in demand for public transport for the first time in several decades. In Denmark, for example, bus travel increased by over 40 per cent between 1980 and 1998, while the number of rail passengers in the UK grew by almost 30 per cent over the period 1986 to 2001. In the USA too, public transport has registered growth for the first time in many years and outstripped the growth in car use in both 1999 and 2000. So why is public transport suddenly becoming more popular?

Congestion and pollution are two reasons why many people are returning to public transport. In some of the most congested cities public transport is now the fastest way to get around. For example, in the city of Manila in the Philippines it takes about 15 minutes to travel 22 kilometres using the tramway, a journey that by motor car would take up to 2 hours! Such differences are achieved by giving public transport such as buses and trams their own routes and priority over cars at junctions or traffic lights.

> ## OPINION
> When sufficient people use public transport it makes for more efficient use of space and energy, at far lower cost than private cars, and considerably reduces pollution and greenhouse gas emissions.
>
> Federico Mayor & Jérôme Bindé, The World Ahead, 2001

FRIENDLY DESIGNS

Modern buses and trams have been redesigned to make them more people friendly. They have wider doors for easier and faster boarding, lower floors to ease access for the elderly, disabled or those with young children, and more comfortable seating than in the past. Many systems now include passenger information both at stops and on board the vehicles themselves. This helps people to better plan their journeys and means they know how long they will have to wait before the next service arrives. It has been estimated that around 20 per cent of public transport journey time is taken up by waiting at stops, so any reduction in this will make public transport far more attractive to use.

Video screens at this bus stop in Bangkok, Thailand, provide waiting passengers with information and entertainment.

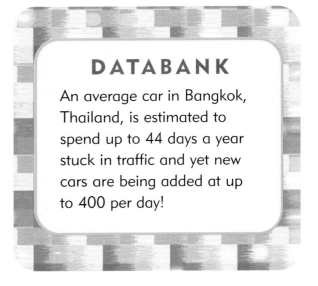

DATABANK

An average car in Bangkok, Thailand, is estimated to spend up to 44 days a year stuck in traffic and yet new cars are being added at up to 400 per day!

Better integration of different transport systems has also helped make public transport more user friendly. In cities such as Vienna (Austria), London (UK) and Stockholm (Sweden) a single ticket allows passengers to transfer between transport modes (such as trains, buses and light railway) for each stage of their journey.

LIGHT RAILWAYS

Among the fastest growing forms of sustainable transport are light rail systems. These are rail systems that run above ground using tracks sunk into existing roads or, alternatively, on especially elevated tracks. These elevated systems are sometimes referred to as sky-trains and operate in Vancouver (Canada), London (UK) and Kuala Lumpur (Malaysia) to name a few. Many of the most advanced light rail systems now operate automatically. Two of the oldest such systems operate in Kobe (Japan) and in Lille (France). The Lille system began service in 1983 and today carries over 230,000 passengers per day. The computer automation means it is punctual and reliable with services departing every five minutes and once a minute during peak times. Safety has also been improved using driverless trains as most accidents on such transport systems tend to be due to driver error.

One advantage of light rail is that, because it runs above ground, it costs less to build than an underground (metro) system. This means light rail has been especially popular for smaller or less wealthy cities. In Germany, for example, more than fifty cities have light rail systems. In less developed countries, cities such as Bangkok, Kuala Lumpur and Manila (The Philippines) all have successful and expanding systems. More cities are now turning to light rail as a part of their solution to transport congestion. In the UK, Nottingham is one of the latest cities to do this. When it opens in 2003, the Nottingham Express Transit (NET) will take an estimated two million car journeys off the city's roads every year.

In cities of over 1 million people, however, full size underground (metro) systems may be more suitable for mass transit than a light rail system. The New York metro system (called the subway in the USA) has been running since 1904 and today operates 6,500 services a day, carrying 3.1 million passengers on 25 interconnected lines. The metros in Moscow (Russia) and Tokyo, though newer, each carry over 7.5 million passengers per day! Both metro and light rail systems require heavy investment and a reliable electricity supply. This means they are not always suitable for less developed countries.

Tokyo's highly efficient metro system carries over 2,700 million passengers per year.

BACK TO THE BUSES

Buses are the most widely used form of public transport with around one billion journeys being made globally every day. Buses are more flexible than rail systems because they do not require great investment in infrastructure (rails, signals, platforms etc) and can run on even the bumpiest of dirt roads. In many less developed countries buses are the main form of intercity transport departing numerous times a day and stopping to pick up and drop off people on demand. Smaller buses (often minibuses) then transfer people from the main bus route and take them to smaller settlements or isolated locations. Such systems work well and provide people with an affordable means of travel.

Buses can also provide effective city transport, though this normally depends on how free their route is kept. In many cities, buses now have their own lanes and priority at junctions and signals. Making bus travel faster can attract people away from their cars. One of the best examples of bus priority comes from Curitiba in Brazil. There, central bus expressways provide quick and reliable transport to all areas of the city along five central corridors. Cars are kept to the edge of the corridors so that there is no congestion or delays for the buses. This simple priority system, combined with modern bus design and flat rate charges, means that almost

70 per cent of Curitiba's population use the buses each day.

In rural areas scheduled bus services are not always an efficient form of transport. Buses can run their entire route with very few passengers and may not go to where passengers need them. In the remote highlands of Scotland new flexible bus routes have been introduced so that passengers can request to be picked up or dropped off at locations close to, but not always on the main route. 'Dial-a-Bus' schemes have also been introduced for people to arrange collection by the nearest available vehicle at a time that suits them best. Such systems make better use of available transport resources, a key priority for a more sustainable future.

DATABANK

Curitiba's highly organized bus transit system can carry an incredible 2 million passengers per day!

In Curitiba, Brazil, buses have their own priority transport route whilst cars are kept to separate outside lanes.

Following local government intervention, many commuters and city residents in Freiburg, Germany, now prefer to travel by bicycle.

PEDAL POWER

Besides walking, cycling is the main form of non-motorized transport used in the world. China alone has over 400 million bicycles and in some cities nearly 80 per cent of journeys are completed by bicycle. In East Africa, bicycle taxis, known as *boda bodas*, are a popular form of transport in non-hilly regions. And it is not just in less developed countries that bicycles are popular. In Denmark around 20 per cent of all journeys are made by bicycle and this rises to 30 per cent in the Netherlands where there are over 19,000 kilometres of cycle tracks.

Priority cycle lanes, the banning of cars from city centres and cycle parking facilities have all contributed to a recent increase in cycling in many European cities. In the German city of Freiburg, for example, cycle lanes were increased from just 29 km in 1970 to over 500 km by 2001 and over 5,000 secure bicycle parking spaces have been provided. This has led to bicycles being used for over a quarter of Freiburg's journeys. The UK and USA have much lower cycle use but are now trying to make cycling a more attractive option. In the USA, an east-coast cycle trail stretching 4,200 km is nearing completion and in the UK the national cycle network had reached over 10,600 km by mid 2002 with a further 5,500 km of routes planned by 2005.

Cycling is not always the most practical form of transport as there are limits to what can be carried and in poor weather the rider is open to the elements. Innovative ideas are helping to overcome such limitations, however. In the London borough of Tower Hamlets, for example, specially adapted rickshaw taxis (based on the Indian models) have been introduced to try to reduce motorized transport by a third. They can carry two adults and a child and come complete with rain hoods and even blankets to cope with the British weather! A specially extended bicycle called an 'ExtraCycle' allows traders in South Africa and Kenya to carry produce to and from market, making it much easier than on a normal bike. The US company that invented the ExtraCycle also sells it in the USA as a Sports Utility Bike, able to carry surfboards, camping equipment, friends, or even pets!

---
weblinks

For more information on the national cycle network in the UK, go to
www.waylinks.co.uk/series/susworld/transport

Pedal rickshaws provide an interesting adaptation of the bicycle and are a relatively quick way of travelling around New York's busy streets.

DATABANK

In the year 2000, world bicycle production climbed to 101 million, more than double the 41 million cars produced.

INTEGRATED TRANSPORT

Many transport systems are planned individually with little thought for the needs of passengers to transfer between different travel modes. In many towns and cities, for example, the central bus station may be some distance from the rail or metro systems. Similarly, facilities for cyclists to safely leave their bicycles are often poor at rail, bus or metro stations. Such conditions can deter people from using public transport and encourage car use as it seems more convenient and faster.

Many transport experts believe that until such problems are resolved it will be difficult to persuade people to leave their cars. They argue that there is a need for integrated transport systems that give public transport networks the same freedom and ease of use that people associate with private motor cars. Many countries are now adopting such approaches and some have already proved very successful. In Stockholm, Sweden, for example, the metro, rail and bus networks operate from a central building allowing easy transfer for passengers between the different transport modes. Clear signs and transferable tickets allow the system to operate with little queuing and waiting time for passengers. Even the ferries that travel between Stockholm's

Travellers arriving at the central station in Stockholm, Sweden, can conveniently choose a train, bus, taxi or coach to continue their journey.

numerous islands are integrated with local bus services that wait to meet the ferry and collect passengers at the main stopping points.

One way to improve use of public transport is to improve timetables for different services so that they are better integrated. Waiting times can make a journey by public transport up to twice as long as by private vehicle. In the Austrian city of Graz, routes, timetable and fares for all forms of public transport are co-ordinated by a single organization. This helps to reduce waiting times and improve journey times significantly. As in Stockholm, a single station provides connections between different transport modes including facilities for cyclists to safely store their bicycles.

Integrated transport in Sweden: a local bus waits for a ferry so that passengers will not have to wait before continuing their journey.

In Germany, the rail network has actively promoted 'bike and rail' services by increasing the space available for cycles to be carried on trains in specially designed compartments. Brochures and a 'bicycle hotline' provide cyclists with information about appropriate services. This helped to double the number of bikes carried on German railways, to over 1.6 million per year within a decade. Caltrain in California introduced a free 'Bikes-on-Board' programme in 1992 and now offers a bike carriage on every commuter train, carrying a total of some 2,000 bicycles per day in 2002.

Making sustainable transport work

CREATING THE TECHNOLOGY and infrastructure to make transport more sustainable is only a small part of the problem. Much harder is the task of convincing people to use such systems as part of their daily travel plans. The dominance of the car has become part of society itself. In countries where car use is currently low, such as China, cars are seen as a symbol of success and their use is growing rapidly. In fact, in many Chinese cities (especially Beijing and Shanghai), preference is being given to improving road networks while existing sustainable transport options such as cycling are being restricted. So what can be done to make sustainable transport work?

PAYING THE PRICE

One of the simplest suggestions to make transport more sustainable is simply to charge according to its real cost. The real cost includes not just the running costs, but also the cost of damage to the environment or people's health. Using such methods, cars and other petrol- or diesel-driven vehicles would become

China is building new roads to encourage car use and preventing cyclists from entering some city centres.

Two-seater Smart cars have ultra-low carbon dioxide emissions and so qualify for lower road taxes in the UK.

relatively expensive to use and people may be encouraged to use alternatives such as public transport or walking and cycling. Introducing such charges is not easy, however. Many governments have adopted alternative ways of charging for less sustainable transport types. In the UK, for example, new cars are taxed according to the amount of carbon dioxide they emit. The cleaner the car the less the annual road tax costs. Taxes on fuel are also used to promote sustainability. In 1989, for example, fuel that contained lead was taxed in the UK to make it more expensive and to persuade people to switch to cheaper and cleaner unleaded petrol. Before the introduction of the tax on leaded fuel, only 1 per cent of vehicles in the UK used unleaded fuel, but within a year of its introduction this had risen to 25 per cent.

Fuel taxes are also said to persuade people not to use their cars, but in the UK where 76 per cent of the fuel price is government tax, car use remains high and traffic is predicted to double by 2025. Elsewhere, governments have introduced more targeted forms of charging to encourage more sustainable transport use and others are now following their example.

> **OPINION**
>
> Taxes on motorists should be tripled to reflect the true cost of road transport, which adds 11 billion pounds a year to health bills because of exhaust pollution.
>
> *The British Lung Foundation 1998*

TARGETED CHARGES

Targeted charges make less sustainable forms of transport more expensive and encourage changes in transport use. In the UK, for example, a driver using a car on quiet rural roads is charged the same road tax as one using it in busy city traffic. Studies show, however, that the cost to society (pollution, health effects, noise, etc) is 25 times higher for the urban driver. By targeting urban drivers, where alternative transport options are normally at their best, it is hoped that urban car traffic can be significantly reduced. From February 2003 cars in London have had to pay £5 a day to enter central areas of the city. A survey in May 2002 suggested that half of London's car drivers would change their travel habits following the introduction of the charge. Similar schemes operating in Singapore and Salzburg, Austria, have been successful in encouraging motorists to switch to public transport or walking and cycling instead. Such schemes are only practical, however, if alternative forms of transport are available. It is the lack of alternatives that makes people critical of such charges.

Car drivers must pay a toll if they wish to travel in Singapore's 'restricted zone' towards the centre of the city.

TRANSPORT EFFICIENCY

Greater transport efficiency is being promoted by several governments. In New Zealand, Iceland, Norway and Sweden, for example, lorries are charged according to the weight they carry and the distance travelled. This promotes the more efficient use of lorries, many of which would otherwise travel around half empty. In the UK, 81 per cent of annual freight traffic is carried by road, but around 30 per cent of the lorries on UK roads are empty at any one time!

Special lanes for high occupancy vehicles (HOVs) are another transport efficiency scheme. These allow vehicles carrying more than one passenger (often a minimum of three) to use a separate lane to other traffic in order to speed up their journey time. In Los Angeles, USA, one of the first cities to introduce HOV lanes in 1973, 35 per cent of the freeways are now set aside for HOVs. Similar schemes operate in forty other North American cities and several Australian ones including Sydney, Melbourne and Brisbane. In the UK, Leeds has been experimenting with HOV lanes since 1998. If successful it could be significant as UK studies have shown that 70 to 80 per cent of car commuters travel on their own – an extremely inefficient form of transport.

Many lorries are empty for some of their journeys and so are an inefficient form of transport.

A theatre group in Seville, Spain, promotes alternative forms of transport during Europe's annual Car Free Day.

PROMOTING ALTERNATIVES

Discouraging people from using motor transport does not always work and can be abused by some motorists. In Los Angeles, for example, people have been caught using inflatable passengers in order to use HOV lanes and fool the authorities. Transport campaigners suggest that there is a need for more direct promotion of alternatives and restraint on motorized traffic if gridlock is to be avoided. Some new ideas are now in practice around the world. These include bans on cars entering city centres; government funding for public transport; and education campaigns to make people aware of their transport choices and the effect they have.

In Europe, for example, the annual 'car free day' started in La Rochelle, France, in 1997. It quickly spread to include over 1,000 towns and cities across the continent by 2001. Each year on 22 September, governments and city/town authorities close down city streets to motorized traffic, and pedestrians and cyclists take over the streets. Events are held to promote awareness of sustainable transport and from 2002 onwards several European cities will extend these activities

Every day thousands of shoppers enjoy walking along car-free Grafton Street in Dublin, Ireland.

as part of the new European Mobility Week (16-22 September). This will raise awareness of public transport services and show the importance of returning cities and streets to the people who live in them and not the motor car.

As we have already learned, several cities have near permanent car-free policies for part or all of the day (see pages 18-19). Where these have been introduced businesses have benefited as more people enjoy the pleasures of shopping and doing business in a cleaner, quieter and safer environment. Zurich in Switzerland is living proof that adopting sustainable transport need not harm the economy as many fear. Yet governments and city authorities often seem reluctant to cut down on car use, believing it will make them unpopular with voters. This can be seen in government spending on transport at a national level. In the USA for example it is estimated that US$108 billion was spent on streets and highways in 1998 compared with just US$26 billion on public transport projects.

weblinks

For more information on the European Mobility Week campaign, go to www.waylinks.co.uk/series/susworld/transport

OPINION

'More and more of Europe's streets are ugly corridors dominated by traffic, noise, parked cars and highway engineering. Let us re-establish them as places where people young or old play, meet, chat, kiss, snooze, drink, eat or walk the dog. We need to turn the tide of motor traffic and create 'living streets'.

European Mobility Week Website 2002

Protestors block a busy street in London during a demonstration to 'Reclaim the Streets'.

PUBLIC OPINION

Despite government fears, recent surveys suggest that many people would be happy to see less car use. In Strasbourg, France, for example, two-thirds of motorists believe that cars in towns will soon become 'a thing of the past' and that the city should rightly belong to pedestrians, cyclists and public transport only. In the UK a recent survey showed that around 40 per cent of people believed transport was the biggest problem in their local area and that the government was not doing enough about it. Over half supported greater use of schemes such as priority bus lanes and a quarter of motorists said they would use the bus if journey times could be reduced.

CHANGING BEHAVIOUR

Such results are encouraging for sustainable transport, but turning them into a reality is much more difficult. One of the greatest challenges is to change people's attitudes and behaviour to public transport, especially in cultures where the car has become such a status symbol. In some countries, car-sharing pools have been introduced to remove the emphasis on everyone having their own vehicle. The car pool owns a number of vehicles. Members can arrange to borrow a car for a short period when they need one. This encourages people to better plan their use of the car for essential journeys only and to walk for journeys over shorter distances. By having different types of vehicles available in the pool, members can also select the most appropriate vehicle for each use.

Italy is the latest country to join the European Car Sharing Association with fleets of electric vehicles in several cities including Rome and Milan. Customers are given a magnetic card and can collect one of the electric cars from special parking areas all over the city. They pay for the service according to the distance driven. More than 550 towns are involved in the European Car Sharing Association and by 2003 it is predicted to have over 350,000 car-sharers. Such schemes show how relatively small changes in personal behaviour (simply giving up personal car ownership) can make great contributions towards sustainable transport.

Providing car parking for commuters and city residents uses up enormous areas of valuable urban land.

DATABANK

Studies have shown that an average car may be parked up for as much as 95 per cent of its lifetime.

Sustainable transport and you

Each of us must take personal responsibility for our own transport choices if a sustainable transport future is to become a reality. It is of little use complaining about pollution, congestion, poor health and environmental damage if each time we go to school, work or the shops we hop into the family car.

A 'walking bus' scheme in England gets younger children safely to school.

TAKING IT PERSONALLY

A study in Grenoble, France, found that 50 per cent of children living within 400 m of their school and 80 per cent of children living within 800 m travelled there each day by car!

OPINION

Parents are rightly worried about the safety of their kids on our crowded roads. But putting even more children into cars is not the answer. It's bad for the environment, bad for their health, and can threaten the safety of others. Walking Bus schemes could be the answer...

Tanya Jowett, Friends of the Earth, Maidenhead, UK

To reduce these figures, 'walking-bus' and 'cycling-bus' schemes were introduced. These provide safe routes for children to get to school whereby volunteers (normally parents) take it in turns to accompany a group of children to and from school by either walking or cycling. One volunteer is the 'driver' (at the front) and the other the 'conductor' (at the back) and the route can be varied to pick up and drop off children along the way. Similar schemes also operate in the UK, New Zealand, USA and Canada and have been shown to not only reduce traffic, but to increase the health of the children involved.

You can take responsibility for your own transport choices by choosing the most sustainable method possible. This will often be walking or cycling. In the UK, for example, a quarter of all car journeys are less than 2 km – easy walking distance for most people. Where longer journeys are necessary, find out about public transport options, or at the very least try to share your journey with others if you have to go by car.

One type of travel you have little choice over is if you fly somewhere for your holiday. However even this can be made more responsible by paying a small fee to offset the carbon dioxide emitted during your flight. A company called 'Climate Care' will invest your payment into projects that neutralize carbon-dioxide emissions such as tree planting or distributing low-energy light bulbs. At just £0.95 per hour of air travel for each person this scheme adds only £30 to the cost of an average family holiday – not much for a more sustainable future.

Passengers checking in at Hamburg airport in Germany could pay a voluntary tax to reduce the environmental impact of their flight.

weblinks

To find out more about 'Climate Care', go to
www.waylinks.co.uk/series/susworld/transport

These passengers on the Eurostar train service between the UK and mainland Europe have time and space to enjoy a meal, read a book, or just relax and enjoy the scenery.

When you become an adult you will have even more power to make your transport choices sustainable. For example, by choosing where to live and work you can minimize the need for travel in the first place, and you can make sure that if you need to travel you have access to public transport services. If you live in an area with good transport links you may want to think twice before getting a driving licence. Do you really need it? Think of all the money you could save in tax, fuel and garage costs! If you travel long distances with your family then think about using the train. By planning ahead you can normally get guaranteed seats and cheaper fares. You could even plan your family holiday by rail, bus or boat as a more sustainable way to travel than by air. It can also be more relaxing with time to enjoy the scenery or read a good book.

DON'T LOOK BACK!

Most importantly you should act now so that you don't look back in several years' time and wonder how the world around you has become even more congested and polluted than it used to be. The examples in this book show that there are transport alternatives that not only bring us personal freedom, but also a cleaner, healthier and more people-friendly environment in which to live. This is surely what we want not only for ourselves, but for future generations – your children and grandchildren.

For short distances and local travel, bicycles are a healthy, fun, quick and easy choice.

LOCAL ACTION
Doing your bit

There are many different ways in which you can contribute to sustainable transport. Here are just a few ideas to get you started.

- Think before you travel and use the most sustainable method available.

- Find out about public transport in your area.

- Walk or cycle to school, or join a walking- or cycling-bus scheme.

- Share lifts with friends and other family members if you use the car.

- Join a group campaigning for more sustainable transport.

- If you have a family car, make sure it is as efficient as possible.

- Work with your school to improve transport options to and from school.

- Find out about home delivery shopping or travelling services such as libraries.

- Share your knowledge about sustainable transport with friends and family.

The future of sustainable transport

EXAMPLES FROM AROUND THE WORLD show us what a future focused on sustainable transport might look like and many of these have been featured in this book. We have also seen the importance of government and individual commitments to improving transport choices and learned how we can each do our own bit. Despite these positive examples, we are faced with a world that is becoming ever more congested and polluted by the dominance of motorized transport and its reliance on fossil fuels.

A driver recharges the batteries of his electric car in Germany using sustainable energy provided by solar panels.

HOPEFUL SIGNS

There are signs that governments, businesses and individuals around the world are finally getting serious about transport issues. Major car companies are investing in cleaner technology such as hydrogen fuel cell vehicles (see pages 16-17) , and many businesses are doing their bit to improve their own transport needs such as using electric vehicles or providing better facilities for cyclists. The best

As more people use public transport like these German trams, so the service will improve for the future.

signals come from those cities where the private motor car is being rejected in favour of public transport and greater access for people. These cities, such as Zurich in Switzerland, Freiburg in Germany and Copenhagen in Denmark, are the best indication yet that sustainable transport can bring about a better future for all.

IN YOUR HANDS

In truth, though, the future of sustainable transport is in the hands of individuals such as you and I. New technology and government policies can provide us with the tools and incentives for sustainable transport, but whether or not these are turned into a reality will depend on our personal choices. As citizens, we have the power to influence businesses and governments through the decisions we make, the schemes we support, and the problems that we stand up to. The more that public transport is used, for example, the more likely companies are to invest in new routes or more frequent services. In turn this is likely to increase the appeal of public transport to others.

You also have the power to influence others by educating them about sustainable transport and encouraging them to make better transport choices. Each of us must take this responsibility seriously if we are to develop transport systems for life in more sustainable world.

Glossary

Acid rain Produced when pollutants such as sulphur dioxide and nitrogen oxides (emitted when fuels are burned) mix with water vapour in the air.

Aerodynamic A shape that is designed to reduce the effects of air resistance.

Climate change The process of long-term changes to the world's climate (warming or cooling, etc). Occurs naturally, but today is more as a result of human activities polluting the atmosphere.

Congestion Where vehicles overcrowd a street or road making movement difficult or impossible for some time.

Developed countries The wealthier countries of the world including Europe, USA, Canada, Japan, Australia and New Zealand.

Emissions Polluting waste products (gas and solids) released into the atmosphere. These include carbon, sulphur and lead from car exhaust fumes.

Ethanol A colourless liquid, produced from fermented carbohydrates such as sugar cane.

Fossil fuels Fuels from the fossilized remains of plants and animals formed over millions of years. They include coal, oil and natural gas.

Fuel efficiency Whereby improvements in vehicle design and fuel mean that vehicles can travel further on the same amount of fuel.

Global warming The gradual warming of the earth's atmosphere as a result of greenhouse gases, such as carbon dioxide and methane, trapping heat.

Gridlock When congestion affects a wider area than usual so that vehicles are unable to move in any direction at all.

Infrastructure Networks that enable communication and/or people, transport and the economy to function: such as roads, railways, electricity, phone lines and pipelines.

Integrated transport systems The co-ordination of different forms of transport (buses, trains, trams, cars etc) to improve people's mobility and reduce pollution in the environment.

Light railway Small-scale railways that run on sunken or elevated tracks.

Mass transit The transition (movement) of large numbers of people.

Metro A railway system in a town or city which runs either wholly or partly underground.

Mobility The ability to move from one location to another, e.g. for leisure or work.

Motorized transport Any form of transport that has a motor fitted to it, but usually means road vehicles.

Non-renewable resources Resources that once used are gone and cannot be replaced except over millions of years. These include coal, oil and natural gas.

Public transport Passenger vehicles, e.g. buses, trains and trams, running on set routes, at set times and fares.

Renewable resources resources that can be re-used through careful management (i.e. replanting forests as they are used) or that are unaffected by human use (i.e. the energy of the sun or wind).

Rite of passage An event that marks a significant time in someone's life.

Road pricing Policy whereby motorists have to pay to use a particular road or section of it.

Smog A mixture of fog, smoke and air borne pollutants such as exhaust fumes.

Sports utility vehicle (SUV) A vehicle (normally four-wheel-drive), designed specially for use on rough ground, but used mostly for everyday driving.

Sustainable transport Transport systems which meet the needs of today's global population without causing harm to people or the environment, both now and in the future.

Zero emission Vehicles, such as bicycles, that do not release any polluting waste products.

Books to read

21st Century Debates: Transportation by Rob Bowden (Hodder Wayland 2004)

Children's Encyclopedia of Transport: on the Move by Andrew Nahum (Marshall Editions, 2001)

Earth Alert!: Transport by Andrew Church and Amanda Church (Hodder Wayland, 2001)

Environment Starts Here!: Transport by Angela Royston (Hodder Wayland, 2001)

Great Inventions: Transport by Paul Dowswell (Heinemann Library 2002)

A Century of Change: Transport by Jane Shuter (Heinemann Library, 1999)

Useful Addresses

Friends of the Earth UK
26-28 Underwood Street London N1 7JQ
UK
Tel: 0207 490 1555
www.foe.co.uk

Sustrans (UK)
35 King Street, Bristol BS1 4DZ
UK
Tel: 0117 926 8893
www.sustrans.org.uk

The Centre for Alternative and Sustainable Transport (CAST)
School of Sciences
Mellor Building
College Road
Stoke-on-Trent
Staffordshire ST4 2DE
UK

Tel: 01782 295771
www.staffs.ac.uk/schools/
sciences/geography/cast/

Index

The numbers in **bold** refer to photographs as well as text.